IMAGES
of America

PITT COUNTY
EASTERN REFLECTIONS

LAWYERS AND COUNTY OFFICIALS ON STEPS OF THE PITT COUNTY COURTHOUSE IN GREENVILLE, 1911. These men are as follows: (seated) J.J. Harrington, deputy register of deeds; Alex L. Blow; and W.F. Evans; (first row) Col. Harry Skinner; J.B. James; A.T. Moore, deputy clerk; W.B. Long; and Julian Brown; (second row) Governor Thomas Jordan Jarvis; R.C. Flanagan; C.C. Pierce; S.J. Everett; and W.C. Dresbach, surveyor; (third row) D.C. Moore, clerk, Superior Court; D.M. Clark; C.D. Rountree, justice of the peace; Albion Dunn; Don Gilliam; F.C. Harding; N.W. Outlaw; S.I. Dudley, sheriff; and R. Hyman, deputy sheriff.

IMAGES
of America

PITT COUNTY
EASTERN REFLECTIONS

Mary Boccaccio

ARCADIA
PUBLISHING

Published by Arcadia Publishing
Charleston, South Carolina

Library of Congress Catalog Card Number: 98-86002

For all general information contact Arcadia Publishing at:
Telephone 843-853-2070
Fax 843-853-0044
E-mail sales@arcadiapublishing.com
For customer service and orders:
Toll-Free 1-888-313-2665

Visit us on the Internet at www.arcadiapublishing.com

Note: Credits that read "UA, ECU" refer to the University Archives at East Carolina University. Credits that read "ECMC, ECU" refer to the East Carolina Manuscript Collection, East Carolina University. All other photographs are credited to the person who provided the image.

Contents

Acknowledgments

This volume really belongs to the people who have contributed their photographs and that part of their family history to it. Ralph and Ramona Tucker have kept finding photographs, and when unidentified, they have known which family members to call for the names and dates. These names have been primarily south of Greenville along the New Bern Road. Dorothy Tucker Taft has provided pictures of various family homes and a seventh grade class from East Carolina Teacher's College as part of the Training School program. Blanche Monroe, a friend with whom I have worked on another project, was able to get me started with a friend of hers who had turn-of-the-century photographs. Never shy to ask for help, I asked Charles Ward, who recommended his cousin, Janice White Koonce. Mrs. Koonce not only has a large number of Bethel photographs, but also a number of relatives who have helped identify them. Sarah McPherson has listened to all my difficulties and has suggested people for me to call about the project. James Nelson, one of her suggestions, recommended John Watson Sr., who also has a variety of interesting images. Going back to Greenville Area Preservation Association days, Jack Taft introduced me to the May Museum in Farmville, where Kim Barrow helped me to find photos related to the picking, curing, and sale of tobacco. Hazel Eden had a wonderful photograph of the Chero Cola plant, as well as a number of other pictures. Virginia Perkins volunteered wonderful turn-of-the-century family pictures. Thelma Flye and her niece Judy Beacham have contributed photographs from the farming community of Porter Town and 1950s pictures of businesses in downtown Greenville. Ada Bette Joyner Savage has given a family photograph as well, which highlighted family connections within the community for me. One relative has a photograph and another has a volume of translation from that particular family. Mr. and Mrs. J.B. Joyner have both provided photographs from both sides of their families, and Mr. and Mrs. Rudolph Scheller have contributed an image of a family business on the edge of town 30 years ago. Mr. Laughinghouse has not only contributed pictures, but talked with me about tobacco auctions. Special thanks go to Don Lennon, who began the East Carolina Manuscript Collection over 25 years ago and has been responsible for finding the collection we have.

My own part in the production of this volume has been minimal. I have functioned first as "gofer," that is finding the images to begin with; and second as "expeditor," making sure that all the parts come together when they are supposed to do so. It has been a learning experience for me, one which truly has been my benefit.

Introduction

Two themes come to mind about Pitt County right away, education and tobacco. Because Pitt County is a rural and agricultural county, education has been a concern and a particular focus of its population throughout its history. Small academies began to develop as early as 1814 to combat illiteracy and that thrust to make education available has continued to this day. One of Pitt County's most influential figures in education, Thomas J. Jarvis moved to Pitt County in 1875. Later to become governor (1880–1884) and then ambassador to Brazil (1885–1889), Jarvis had earned tuition for two degrees at Randolph-Macon College by teaching school in the summers. During the early 1900s, he was chairman of the city school board in Greenville, spoke for the establishment of the Teachers Training School in Greenville (1907), and was appointed to the board of trustees of the school once it was established. He oversaw the groundbreaking for the school and was chairman of the executive committee, which was involved in selecting the first president and faculty to open for classes in 1909. The school has grown steadily. In 1921, it became East Carolina Teachers College; in 1951, East Carolina College; and in 1967, East Carolina University. In 1974, a four-year school of medicine opened. The school has grown and prospered through the years.

In the 1860s, Pitt County was a leader in the production of cotton. After the Civil War, cotton became more expensive to grow and harvest, and by the 1880s, cotton prices began to drop. Tobacco was seen by several local farmers as a replacement crop in the late 1880s. In 1891, O.L. Joyner and Alex Heilbroner opened the Eastern Tobacco Warehouse. In 1903, Imperial Tobacco built a plant in town. In 1900, Carolina and Virginia Telephone bought out the local system which had 100 subscribers. The Light, Water and Sewer Company began operation in 1907. The same bond issue which allowed utilities also paved Dickinson and Evans with bricks. In 1908, a steel bridge was built over the Tar River. The town was growing and tobacco has helped it to prosper. Tobacco has been the money crop for the county throughout the twentieth century. In the past 20 years, however, tobacco has developed a progressively bad health profile. The eastern North Carolina leaf is a good product, though, and is one which foreign markets consistently buy to mix in with their own blends. It is likely that tobacco will be grown here well into the future. Cotton has come back as a cash crop in Pitt and surrounding counties and may well become a replacement for tobacco in future decades.

—Mary Boccaccio

One

Home and Family

CELIUS ALLEN TUCKER HOME, SOUTH OF GREENVILLE ON THE NEW BERN ROAD, ABOUT 1898.
Celius Allen "Bob" Tucker and Melissa Cox Tucker are seen in front of their home with, from left to right, Ola Lee, Heber Little, Novella, and William Allen standing in front of the fence. (Courtesy of Jean Tucker Joyner.)

KING FAMILY IN FRONT OF THEIR HOME AT 600 DICKINSON AVENUE IN GREENVILLE, 1918.
The people pictured are, from left to right, as follows: (first row) Amine E. King Galbreath,
Mrs. Richard W. King, and L.W. Gaylord; (second row) Howard Hoskins, Tom A. Galbreath,
Richard W. King Jr., Mattie Moye King Gaylord, Sue Boyd (nurse), and L.W. Gaylord
Jr. (young boy at his mother's knees); (third row) Virginia Dare King, Charles M. King,
Nancy Elizabeth King, Julie Woodson Gaylord, and an unidentified nurse. (Courtesy of
Virginia Perkins.)

H.A. SMITH FARMHOUSE, FARMVILLE AREA, ABOUT 1840. Originally built with pegs, the house
was moved in 1977 from the back of the property to the front and renovated. (Courtesy of
Ralph Chapman Tucker Sr.)

10

TUCKER HOME PLACE, SOUTH OF GREENVILLE. Built in 1914, the house was later moved to Bells Chapel Road. (Courtesy of Ralph Chapman Tucker Sr.)

CATHERINE HARDEE TUCKER, ABOUT 1860. She married William Hardy Tucker in 1850. (Courtesy of Jean Tucker Joyner.)

JEANNETTE RANDOLPH JENKINS, ABOUT 1870. Her family moved from England to Virginia and then to Pitt County, where she married Dr. John H. Jenkins and settled in Penny Hill. (Courtesy of John Watson Sr.)

COX FAMILY, ABOUT 1870. The members of the Cox family in this photograph are, from left to right, as follows: Annie Laurie, Archibald, Ada, Sarah Elizabeth Wilson, Melissa, Leon Herman, and Elizabeth. (Courtesy of Ada Bette Joyner Savage.)

THE LLOYD FAMILY. Seen from left to right, John Maynard and Almyra Whitehurst Lloyd, Brittania Whitehurst, and the Lloyd children—Margaret, Addie, and Jennie—are captured in this 1886 picture in Bethel. (Courtesy of John Watson Sr.)

BIRD'S-EYE VIEW OF GREENVILLE IN THE EARLY 1900S. This image shows some traditional Pitt County homes with detached kitchens and front yards used for growing corn. The Tar River is visible on the extreme left. (Courtesy of ECMC, ECU.)

13

HARVEY, ALLEN, SARAH, AND RUBY EASON, PITT COUNTY, 1909. (Courtesy of Ralph Chapman Tucker Sr.)

CARRIE MYRTLE STOKES EDWARDS IN HER BRIDE'S DRESS NEAR HER HOME IN PORTER TOWN/EASTERN PINES IN 1911. (Courtesy of Thelma Flye.)

THE KING FAMILY IN A CARRIAGE AT THE BACK OF THEIR HOME, READY FOR AN EXCURSION. Richard Jr., Mattie, unidentified, Mattie Moye King, and Richard Warren, from left to right, appear in this c. 1903 picture taken in Greenville. The family "help" is looking on from the back porch. (Courtesy of Virginia Perkins.)

CARRIE CHAPMAN TUCKER AND WILLIAM ALLEN TUCKER AT THEIR HOME ALONG THE NEW BERN ROAD, SOUTH OF GREENVILLE, 1917. (Courtesy of Ralph Chapman Tucker Sr.)

WILLIAM EMMETTE PEADEN, FALKLAND,
ABOUT 1900. (Courtesy of Louis Peaden.)

AUNT DUCK AND CHILD NEAR THE BACK PORCH OF HER HOME, FARMVILLE AREA, 1910S.
Notice the dogs on the stump, the bicycle on the steps, and the swing visible farther down the
yard. (Courtesy of ECMC, ECU.)

FRANCIS MARION DUPREE IN THE COTTON YARD OFF THE SIDE PORCH OF HIS HOME, FARMVILLE AREA, ABOUT 1890. The caption reads, "Daddy and the boys." (Courtesy of ECMC, ECU.)

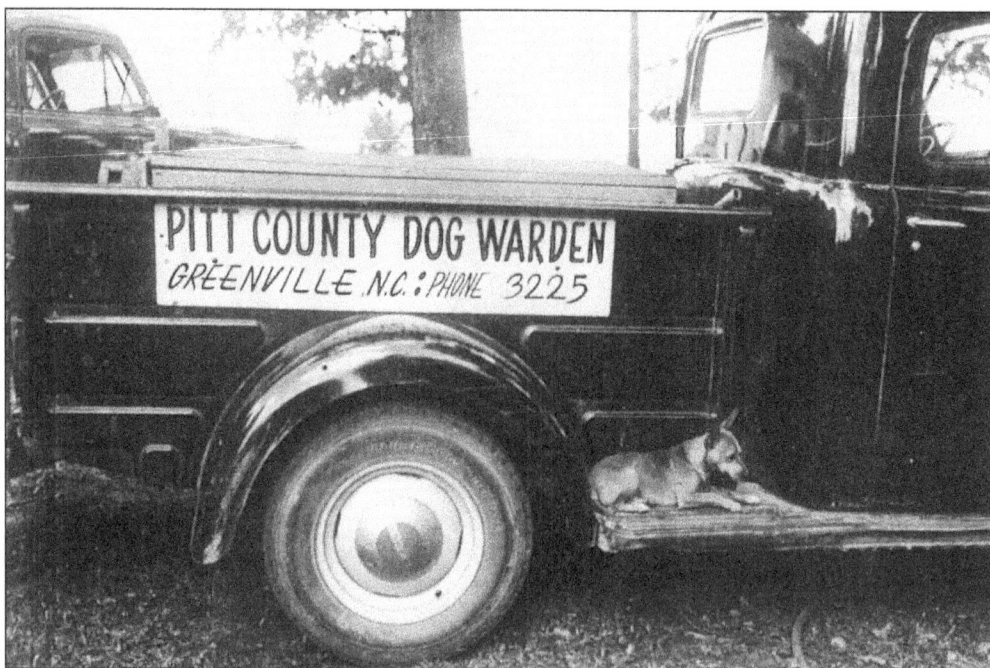

PITT COUNTY DOG WARDEN'S TRUCK. In this 1954 picture taken in Greenville, the warden's dog is seen napping on the running board. (Courtesy of ECMC, ECU.)

18

ELIZABETH SAVAGE, GREENVILLE, 1967. She was an East Carolina Teacher Training School graduate (1918); a third grade teacher at the Evans Street School and Wahl-Coates School, which was an elementary school for training teachers on the campus of East Carolina University; the primary founder of the Pitt County Humane Society; a cruelty investigator for the Humane Society; and a breeder of cocker spaniel and German shepherd dogs. (Courtesy of ECMC, ECU.)

THE FRONT PORCH OF THE OLA L. TUCKER HOME, SOUTH OF GREENVILLE, 1930s. This caption reads, "Our Dogs." (Courtesy of Dorothy Tucker Taft.)

LOUIS MASON EDWARDS FAMILY IN A 1923 STUDEBAKER IN FRONT OF THEIR HOME IN PORTER TOWN. Pictured in the car are, from left to right, the following: Carrie Myrtle Stokes Edwards, Lillian Earl, Louis M. Edwards, Annie Ruth, and Thelma Lee. (Courtesy of Thelma Flye.)

TABITHA MARIE DEVISCONTI, AUNT SUE ALBRITTON, AND SUE MAY DEVISCONTI (FROM LEFT TO RIGHT). These two young sisters are shown with their aunt in an upper-story window of the Albritton home in Farmville in 1908. (Courtesy of ECMC, ECU.)

FARMVILLE BUSINESS DISTRICT ON PINE STREET, C. 1915. (Courtesy of ECMC, ECU.)

EVANS STREET, 1900S. In this view, Evans Street appears as an unpaved residential street with a sidewalk and electric poles lining it. Horse and buggy are visible down the street. (Courtesy of ECMC, ECU.)

RESIDENCE OF MRS. A. SUGG AND HER SISTER, MISS M.M. HEARNE, GREENVILLE, 1910S. (Courtesy of ECMC, ECU.)

LADIES ENTERTAINING ON THEIR FRONT PORCH IN FARMVILLE, C. 1920. (Courtesy of the May Museum.)

THE WARD FAMILY, 1920S. Luke Lafayette Ward (seated on the left), James Harvey Ward (seated on the right), and Wadie Thurman Ward (standing) are photographed here on their porch in Bethel. (Courtesy of Janice White Koonce.)

A THREE-PANEL POSTCARD OF THE TAR RIVER. This *c.* 1908 postcard captures upstream

activities on the river in West Greenville, the Tar River Bridge, and the river downstream. (Courtesy of ECMC, ECU.)

GEORGE ROSCOE WHITFIELD AND FAMILY ON FRONT STEPS OF THEIR HOME, GRIMESLAND, c. 1930. Whitfield opened the County Training School, which was a black farm life school started in 1917 in Grimesland. Seated with Whitfield are his wife, Ester Cherry, and their children: Willie Roscoe, George Raymond, James Herman, Mary Ester, and Beulah Louise. (Courtesy of ECMC, ECU.)

R.L. Davis & Bros. Store on Main Street, Farmville, 1927. A terrific snowstorm plagued the county that year with snow that reached waist deep. Arthur Tugwell is pictured here in front of the store. (Courtesy of the May Museum.)

Joanne Godwin near Her Home at 1012 West Ward Street, Greenville, c. 1930. (Courtesy of Jeanne Jenkins.)

HARRY R. JOYNER ON A FORDSON-MAKE TRACTOR, GREENVILLE, 1938. (Courtesy of J.B. Joyner.)

WATER AND UTILITY COMPANY HUTS FOR STORAGE OF COAL ON THE SOUTH BANK OF THE TAR RIVER IN WEST GREENVILLE. The river was frozen in 1936. This photograph was taken by Paul Flye, an employee of the company. (Courtesy of Thelma Flye.)

28

Siblings Betty and Charles Godwin in front of Their Home on Ward Street in Greenville, 1943. (Courtesy of Jeanne Jenkins.)

Etna Lewis with Niece Cornelia Darden and Ducks in front of the Lewis Home near Farmville, 1953. (Courtesy of Lou Ellen Lewis Rook.)

SUNDAY REUNION OF THE FRENCH, MIZELLE, GRUBBS, ADAMS, DECLUE, AND NEAL FAMILIES, NORTH OF GREENVILLE, 1956. (Courtesy of Jeanne Jenkins.)

ROBERT BURTON GREENE HOME, WEST OF GREENVILLE, SPRINGTIME 1959. (Courtesy of Dorothy Tucker Taft.)

Two

At Work

HEBERT LITTLE TUCKER IN
FRONT OF HIS BLACKSMITH SHOP,
SOUTH OF GREENVILLE, C. 1910.
(Courtesy of Jean Tucker Joyner.)

31

JOHN FLANAGAN BUGGY CO., INC. EMPLOYEES IN FRONT OF THEIR SHOP ON THE CORNER OF FOURTH AND COTANCHE STREETS IN GREENVILLE, 1902. The employees are, from left to right, as follows: Mr. Sutton (Wood Shop), Mr. D.D. Gardner (foreman of the Trimming Room), Mr. W.E. Hoker, Mr. Edward Gaskill Flanagan, Mr. Will Gardner, Lewis Johnson, Bill Smith (Wood Shop), Jimmy Reeves, and Roscoe Jefferson. (Courtesy of ECMC, ECU.)

JOHN FLANAGAN BUGGY CO., INC. CARRIAGE SHOWROOM IN GREENVILLE, C. 1902. (Courtesy of ECMC, ECU.)

JOHN FLANAGAN BUGGY CO., INC. MODEL T SHOWROOM IN GREENVILLE, C. 1920. Flanagan became a Ford dealership in 1914. (Courtesy of Hazel Eden.)

THE CHERO COLA PLANT, LOCATED AT 706 DICKINSON AVENUE IN GREENVILLE, 1918. The president was W.J. Hardee; vice president, R.T. Cox; and secretary/treasurer, C.M. Warren. Coon Williams was the truck driver. (Courtesy of Hazel Eden.)

HOME FURNITURE COMPANY IN GREENVILLE, 1910s. The company sold cookstoves, heaters, and ranges, and this was one of their advertisements on the back of a tobacco sale sheet. (Courtesy of ECMC, ECU.)

Member Federal Deposit Insurance Corp.

1901   Time Tested   1938

For Cook Stoves and Ranges, both coal and wood Stoves, also Oil Stoves or any type of Heater, we have them. We buy them in car-load lots, and you will find our prices lower than the quality.

ENTERPRISE FORESTER STEEL BOX
FOR WOOD

Body made of heavy first quality steel well protected with sectional cast linings. Cast top with swing section and ornamental swing and nickel urn. Heavily corrugated cast iron bottom extra deep with large clear-out door having nickel screw draft register. Cast front with large fire door fitted with mica. Two nickel foot rails. Reversible pipe collar for convenient installation.

HOME FURNITURE STORE
"GOOD FURNITURE AT RIGHT PRICES"

Greenville, N. C.

BETHEL HOTEL STATIONERY LOGO, BETHEL, 1886. (Courtesy of ECMC, ECU.)

35

STANDARD SERVICE STATION, GASOLINE AND MOTOR OIL. Jesse Carraway (far right) and Ed Davenport (left) appear in this 1920s picture taken in Farmville. (Courtesy of the May Museum.)

CHESTER ERASTUS GOLDEN ISACAN HARRIS (STANDING IN FRONT) WITH RALPH C. TUCKER SR. (BEHIND). Seen in this 1924 photograph, Harris was a jack-of-all-trades on the Tucker farm, south of Greenville. (Courtesy of Ralph C. Tucker Sr.)

R.R. Newton (Left) and A.A. Ruffin in a Car in front of Parker and Newton Drug Store in Farmville, 1920s. (Courtesy of ECMC, ECU.)

Parker and Newton Drug Store Soda Fountain, Farmville, 1920s. (Courtesy of ECMC, ECU.)

JENESS MORRILL JR., PROPRIETOR OF RED FEATHER POULTRY FARM, FALKLAND, 1930s. (Courtesy of ECMC, ECU.)

BABY CHICKS TO BE SOLD AT THE POULTRY FARM, FALKLAND, 1930s. (Courtesy of ECMC, ECU.)

DEPRESSION-ERA HOOVER CARTS, FARMVILLE AREA, 1930S. These carts had automobile wheels and a shaft which was attached to a mule and a seat. (Courtesy of the May Museum.)

THE *GENERAL PUTNAM* AT THE GREENVILLE PORT TERMINAL DOCK, 1941. The *Putnam* and other river vessels provided transportation for goods up and down the Tar River. (Courtesy of ECMC, ECU.)

THE GREENVILLE PORT TERMINAL AREA AND THE *EMELINE* AT DOCK, 1941. (Courtesy of ECMC, ECU.)

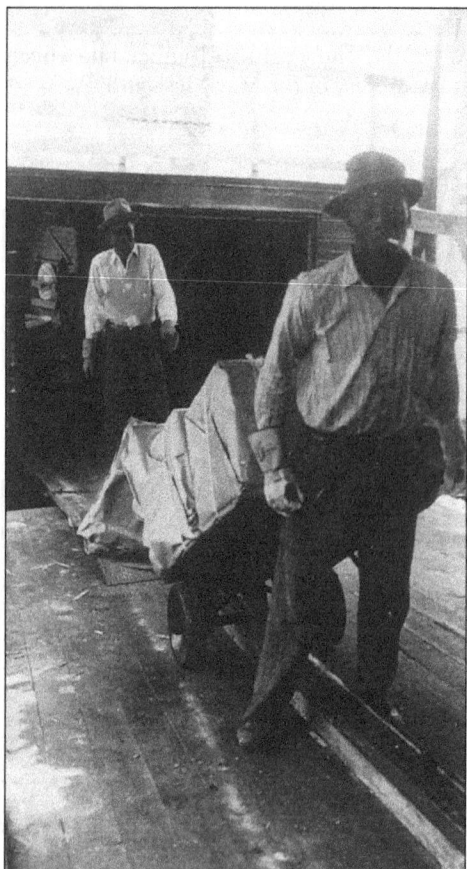

PORTERS UNLOADING A SHIP AT THE PORT TERMINAL, 1941. (Courtesy of ECMC, ECU.)

GREENVILLE WATER AND ELECTRIC PLANT, WEST GREENVILLE, 1908. (Courtesy of ECMC, ECU.)

JOHN WATSON SR. ON THE JOB FOR GREENVILLE UTILITIES, 1930s. (Courtesy of John Watson Sr.)

ELBERT'S PALACE AT 5 DECK STREET, LOCATED "OVER THE HILL" IN GREENVILLE, 1948. This image was taken by John Warner, who was filming a movie in Greenville, on 35-mm film and was later made into a photographic print by Patrick Keough. (Courtesy of Alex Albright.)

CITY TAXI ON THE CORNER OF ALBEMARLE AND WEST FIFTH STREETS, GREENVILLE, 1948. Prince Hemby drove the cab. This image was taken by John Warner on 35-mm film, and the photographic print, by Patrick Keough. (Courtesy of Alex Albright.)

COLONY THEATER AT 420 SOUTH EVANS STREET IN GREENVILLE, 1950s. The theater was playing *The Greatest Show on Earth*. (Courtesy of Judy Beacham.)

JIM'S BILLIARDS, QUICK LUNCH AT 427 SOUTH EVANS STREET IN GREENVILLE, 1950s. (Courtesy of Judy Beacham.)

BISSETTE'S DRUG STORE AT 416 SOUTH EVANS STREET IN GREENVILLE, 1950s. (Courtesy of ECMC, ECU.)

LUNCH COUNTER AT BISSETTE'S, 1950s. At Bissette's Drug Store, many passersby would stop for coffee or a sandwich and see their friends. (Courtesy of ECMC, ECU.)

JUDY EVANS IN FRONT OF MARY ANN SODA SHOP, LOCATED AT 426 SOUTH EVANS STREET IN GREENVILLE, 1950S. (Courtesy of Judy Beacham.)

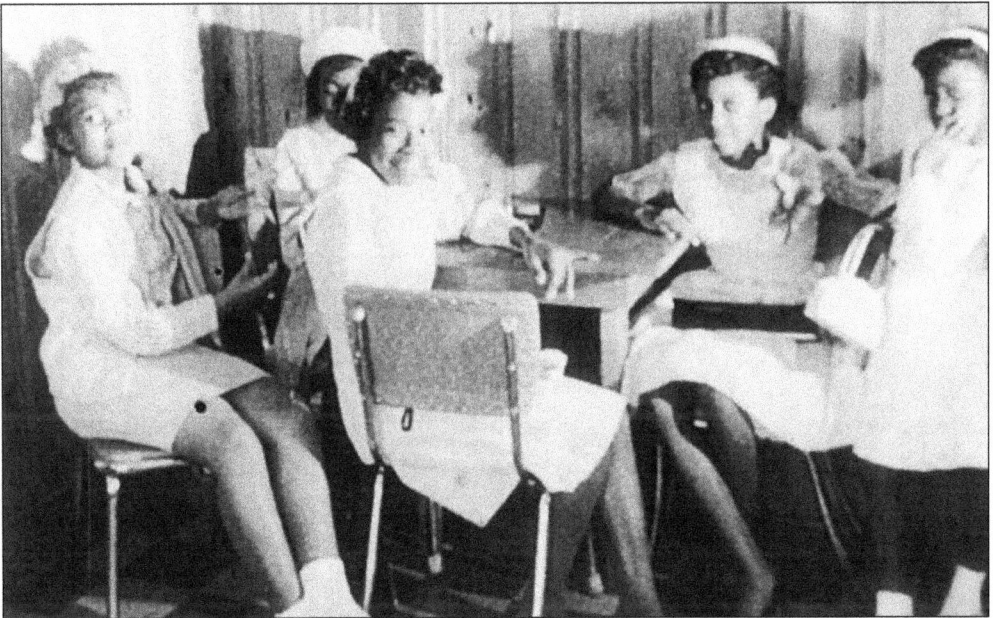

SUNDAY MORNING AT ELBERT'S PALACE, LOCATED AT 5 DECK STREET IN GREENVILLE, 1948. This image was taken by John Warner on 35-mm film, and the photographic print, by Patrick Keough. (Courtesy of Alex Albright.)

GARRIS FURNITURE, LOCATED AT 505–507 DICKINSON AVENUE IN GREENVILLE, 1948. This image was taken by John Warner on 35-mm film, and the photographic print, by Patrick Keough. (Courtesy of Alex Albright.)

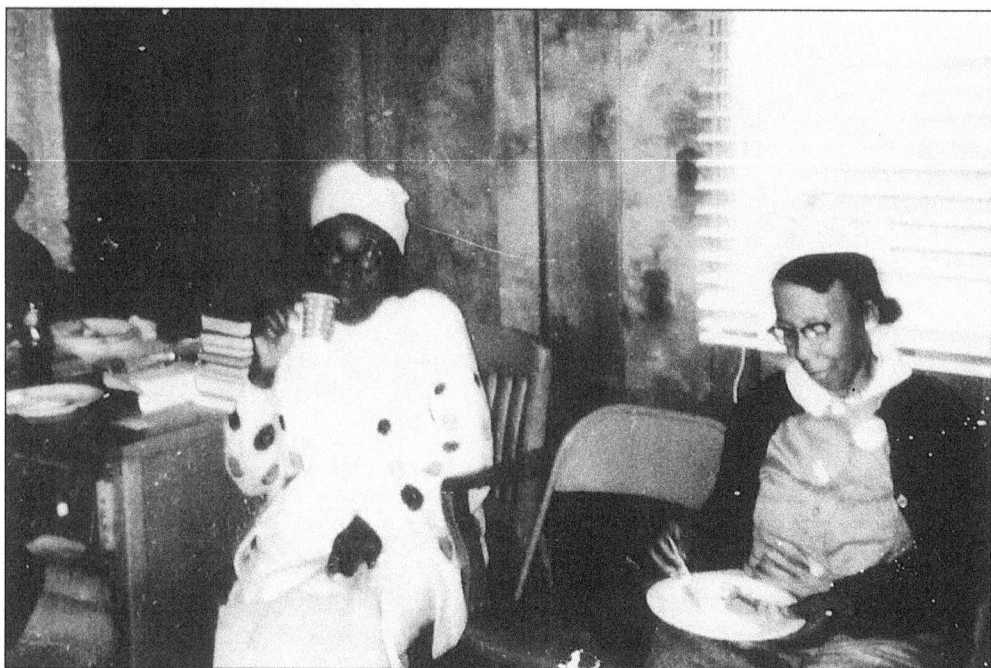

BESSIE WARD HARRIS (RIGHT), A MIDWIFE IN PITT COUNTY FOR 37 YEARS. She was licensed about 1950. Herbalist and practitioner of natural medicine, Miss Bessie "caught" over 1,000 babies. (Courtesy of ECMC, ECU.)

WILLIAM JOSEPH FRENCH SR., 1946.
He appears ready to get into his
appliance repair truck in front of his
home at 100 North Summit Street.
(Courtesy of Jeanne Jenkins.)

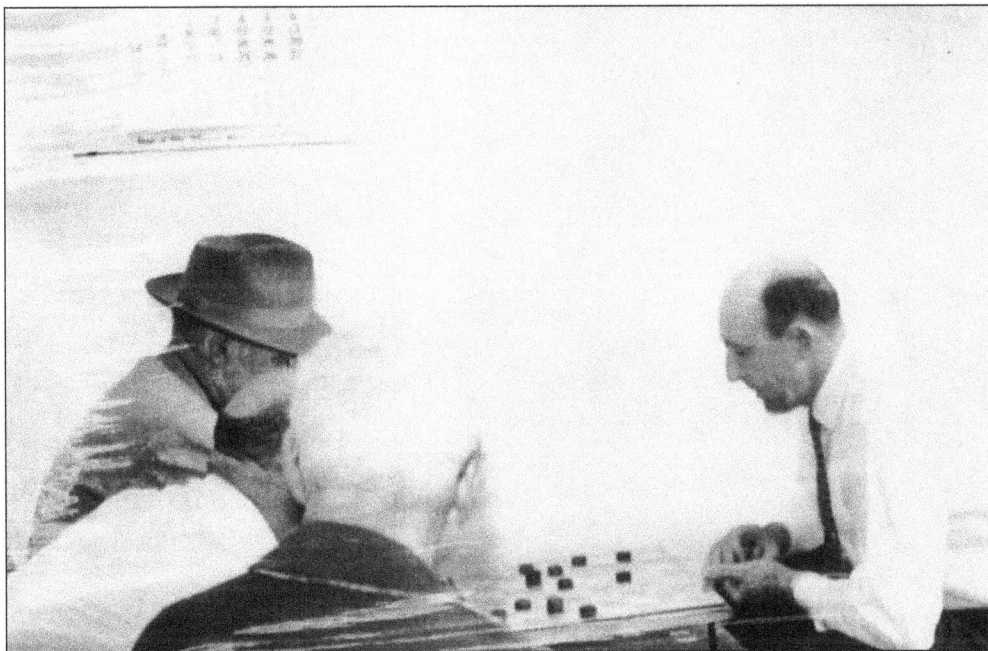

GAME OF CHECKERS AT BOYD'S BARBER SHOP, LOCATED AT 1008 SOUTH EVANS STREET AT
THE CORNER OF FOURTEENTH IN GREENVILLE, 1950S. Depending on the weather, the game was
either inside or out. (Courtesy of Hazel Eden.)

GREENVILLE FULL-FASHIONED HOSIERY MILL, LOCATED AT FOURTEENTH STREET BETWEEN CHARLES STREET AND ARLINGTON BOULEVARD, 1950S. (Courtesy of Hans Scheller.)

REAL CRISIS INTERVENTION CENTER. Some volunteers are pictured here in front of their first location at 570 Cotanche and Eighth Streets. In 1970, some students at East Carolina University asked professors to advise them about ways to help students involved with drugs and a variety of other social problems. A community advisory board was formed which included professors, a variety of socio-medical professionals, and businessmen. A program of training counselors began under the leadership of trained clinical psychologists, who screened volunteers. In 1976, REAL was accepted as a United Way program and also began Dial-a-Teen and a Rape Victims Counseling program. REAL provides 24-hour-a-day service, 7 days a week, 365 days a year either by telephone or on a walk-in basis. (Courtesy of REAL Crisis Intervention Center.)

Three

Flue-Cured Tobacco

EASTERN TOBACCO WAREHOUSE LETTERHEAD LOGO. O.L. Joyner was the owner and proprietor in 1895. Joyner, born in Farmville, moved to Greenville and began warehousing. His system of progressively increasing the size of his warehouses made Greenville a player in the eastern North Carolina tobacco market. (Courtesy of ECMC, ECU.)

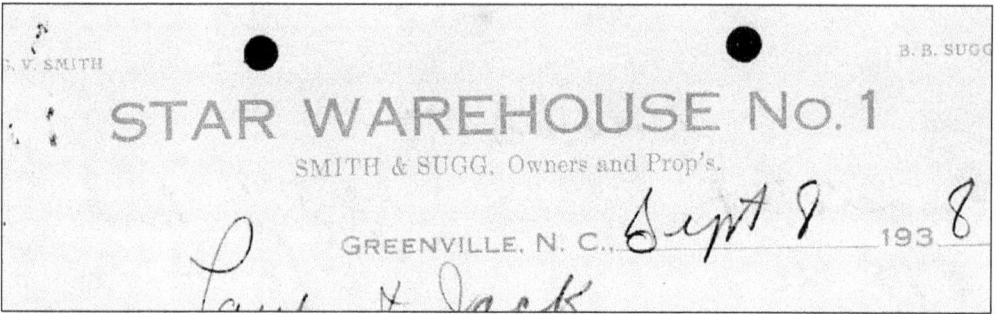

STAR WAREHOUSE SALE SHEET LOGO, GREENVILLE, 1890S. This is one of a number of warehouses that mushroomed in Pitt County in response to the Greenville tobacco market. (Courtesy of ECMC, ECU.)

MONK WAREHOUSE, FARMVILLE, C. 1910. Auction day always was a joyful occasion because farmers would realize the fruits of their labor amid all the excitement and speculation of the crowd that came to watch the festivities. (Courtesy of ECMC, ECU.)

COTTON FIELD WITH TOBACCO BARNS IN THE BACKGROUND, FARMVILLE AREA, 1930s. Cotton was part of a three-crop rotation system which included tobacco and corn. (Courtesy of the May Museum.)

HARVEY AND WADIE WARD IN THEIR TOBACCO FIELD, BETHEL AREA, 1931. (Courtesy of Janice White Koonce.)

WGTC, THE TOBACCO NETWORK.
This radio station was part of the Mutual Broadcasting System and was located on West Fifth Street in Greenville, past Memorial Drive. Owned by Julian J. White in the 1930s, it was purchased by a small group of investors in 1948 who applied to the Federal Communications Commission to have a television channel assigned to eastern North Carolina. Permission was granted in 1951; construction was begun in 1952; and in December 1953, Channel 9 began operations with a primary affiliation to the CBS Network. (Courtesy of Haywood Dail Laughinghouse Jr.)

AN EARLY SPRAYER USED FOR INSECT AND SUCKER CONTROL, PARTICULARLY HORNWORM AND BLOODWORM, FARMVILLE, 1960s. (Courtesy of the May Museum.)

Picking Tobacco, 1954. Here are workers and attendants in the field in the Greenville area. (Courtesy of ECMC, ECU.)

Farmers Loading Tobacco into a Cart to Take to a Bulk Barn, Farmville Area, 1960s. Having a car in the field began around the time of the early bulk barns. (Courtesy of the May Museum.)

Tying Tobacco, Greenville Area, 1954. Farmers and help tied tobacco to sticks so that it could be hung in a tobacco barn for curing, or drying. (Courtesy of ECMC, ECU.)

Stacks of Tobacco Sticks, Farmville, 1950s. Tobacco sticks were stacked in a pile outside of a warehouse, and the warehouses would loan these sticks to farmers. (Courtesy of the May Museum.)

BACKBREAKING WORK, GREENVILLE AREA, 1954. Tobacco workers hand sticks to other help in the barn who arrange the sticks in rows from the top to the bottom of the tobacco barn for curing. (Courtesy of ECMC, ECU.)

A BULK BARN, FARMVILLE, 1960s. An early bulk barn around Farmville had a larger area, so more tobacco at a time could be cured than the smaller tobacco barns. (Courtesy of the May Museum.)

FARMERS LINING UP ALONG THE ROAD TO BRING THEIR TOBACCO TO THE MARKET, FARMVILLE, 1930s. (Courtesy of the May Museum.)

FARMER'S DAY FESTIVAL IN GREENVILLE, 1954. The festival generally coincided with the time the markets opened. The *Daily Reflector* estimated 9,000 people attended festival events that year. (Courtesy of ECMC, ECU.)

KEEL'S WAREHOUSE

GREENVILLE, N. C., _____ 193___

SOLD FOR _Jackson_ _____

N.º 33

IDEN. NO. _____

PRICE   AMOUNT

TOBACCO TIED IN BUNDLES IN THE WAREHOUSE PRIOR TO SALE, FARMVILLE. The practice of tying in bundles stopped in the late 1950s. (Courtesy of the May Museum.)

BAGGED TOBACCO, FARMVILLE, 1960s. Bagged tobacco sits on the warehouse floor until it is untied just before the sale. (Courtesy of the May Museum.)

A CLOSE-UP VIEW ON THE AUCTION FLOOR, FARMVILLE, 1960S. The auctioneer (the man at center in the white shirt with his left arm extended) sings out the sale price to the recorder (with the notepad). Farmers and buyers gather close, inspecting the quality of the sale and noting the prices. (Courtesy of the May Museum.)

AUCTION DAY, FARMVILLE, 1960s. The market floor shows open bundles on baskets. Farmers are walking down the aisle to see what the year's crop looks like. (Courtesy of the May Museum.)

JAMES AND NATHAN COBB MAKING HOGSHEADS TO TRANSPORT THE TOBACCO TO PROCESSING PLANTS, FARMVILLE, 1960s. Hogsheads could hold up to 1,000 pounds of tobacco and were made round so that they could be rolled. (Courtesy of the May Museum.)

Four

Education

TURN-OF-THE-CENTURY SCHOOL BUS, FALKLAND. Falkland is a small community west of Greenville. (Courtesy of ECMC, ECU.)

61

WINTERVILLE ACADEMY STUDENTS, C. 1900. Beginning operations in 1895, the school was known as Winterville High School by 1901, accepting both day and boarding students. (Courtesy of ECMC, ECU.)

WINTERVILLE ACADEMY FACULTY, C. 1900. In 1901, G.E. Lineberry was principal, and F.C. Nye, assistant. Nye became principal in 1909. Also teaching were John R. Carroll, Miss Dora Cox, Miss V.E. Baushall, Miss Vivian Roberson, and Miss Nettie Liles. (Courtesy of ECMC, ECU.)

RED BANKS SCHOOL, SOUTH OF GREENVILLE NEAR THE NEW BERN ROAD, EARLY 1900S.
Here students and teachers pose in front of the rural school for a photograph. (Courtesy of
ECMC, ECU.)

East Carolina Teachers Training School (ECTTS) Groundbreaking, Greenville, 1908. Ceremony participants included the following: Mrs. Haywood Dail, Mrs. T.J. Jarvis, Mrs. W.T. Lipscomb, Mr. Dink James, Mr. Sam White, Mr. Herbert White, Mr. W.H. Harrington, Mr. Jesse Speight, Mrs. A.M. Moseley, Mrs. Irma Dunn, Mr. Haywood Dail, Gov. Thomas J. Jarvis, Mrs. Ed Evans, Mr. Richard King, Mr. Ed Evans, Mr. D.J. Whichard, Mr. Cecil Cobb, Mr. C.V. York, and Mr. R.J. Cobb. The horse at the left was named Codeen and belonged to Mrs. Dail. (Courtesy of UA, ECU.)

East Carolina Teachers Training School as Envisaged in 1908. This is the design of the campus that the school expected to build along Fifth Street. (Courtesy of ECMC, ECU.)

CLASS DAY GRADUATION, GREENVILLE, 1911. This was the first two-year class to graduate after the school opened its doors. Identifiable in this picture are Robert Wright (first row, left of center) and Governor Jarvis (right of center). (Courtesy of UA, ECU.)

ECTTS CLASSMATES ON A TRIP, 1910s. On the left are Julia and Lizzie Burney; at center is Carrie Chapman; and at right are Lelah Roach and Rosa Whitaker. (Courtesy of Ralph C. Tucker Sr.)

THE AUSTIN BUILDING AT EAST CAROLINA TEACHERS COLLEGE, GREENVILLE, 1940s. The building housed all the original classrooms and administrative offices for the school. The distinctive cupola is well remembered, and a replica has been placed on the campus mall. The building was named after Herbert E. Austin, the first science teacher at the school. (Courtesy of ECMC, ECU.)

THE MODEL SCHOOL, EAST CAROLINA TEACHERS COLLEGE, GREENVILLE, C. 1925. The training school developed a Model School program on campus so that students could have the advantage of a practice environment. (Courtesy of ECMC, ECU.)

TENTH GRADE CLASS, FARMVILLE, 1908. The students are, from left to right, as follows: (seated) Lucy Barrett and Bertha Joyner; (standing) Eli Joyner, David Turnage, Aquilla Turnage, and Professor E.M. Rollins. (Courtesy of ECMC, ECU.)

PITT COUNTY SCHOOL BUS SERVICING THE FARMVILLE AREA, 1920. The bus had a serious accident in the vicinity of Hobgood. (Courtesy of the May Museum.)

THE COUNTY TRAINING SCHOOL. The training school was a black farm life school established in Grimesland in 1917. It was part of the Pitt County School system, and its first principal was George Roscoe Whitfield, a graduate of Lincoln University. He became supervisor of the school in 1920 and also served as the principal of Shivers and St. Peter's Schools. Originally a one-room schoolhouse, the County Training School grew to encompass nine rooms, nine teachers, and have an enrollment of 280 students with an average attendance of 236. Between 1936 and 1961, black elementary and high schools decreased from 59 buildings to 18 buildings, increased the number of teachers from 146 to 228, and increased enrollment from 6,485 students to 8,037 students. Mr. Whitfield was an encouragement and a model for education in his community. (Courtesy of ECMC, ECU.)

HOLLY HILL SCHOOL, NORTH OF GREENVILLE, 1920s. This was a one-room school with 1 teacher and an enrollment of 77—average attendance was 63 students. The building rested on 1 acre. (Courtesy of ECMC, ECU.)

WEST GREENVILLE GRAMMAR SCHOOL, GREENVILLE, 1929. Built in 1924, this school was later named Agnes Fullilove School in 1958 after Ms. Fullilove, who had been a teacher in the system from 1926 to 1967 and principal of the school for 25 years. Identified in this picture is William Joseph French Sr. (third row, second from left). (Courtesy of Jeanne Jenkins.)

PITT COUNTY SCHOOL BUS DRIVERS IN FARMVILLE, 1932. From left to right, they are James Jones, Otis Brock, Charlie Rouse, ? Lewis, ? Moye, and Grimes Lewis. (Courtesy of Lou Ellen Lewis Rook.)

BETHEL HIGH SCHOOL, BETHEL, C. 1922. Identified in this picture is Wadie Ward (second row, center). (Courtesy of Janice White Koonce.)

HOME ECONOMICS BUILDING AT AYDEN SCHOOL, AYDEN, 1920s. (Courtesy of ECMC, ECU.)

CHICOD TEACHERAGE, CHICOD, 1930S. In the early years of the public school educational system, teachers were frequently unmarried young women who moved to a new location for employment. For their convenience, teacherages were available for them as boardinghouses. (Courtesy of ECMC, ECU.)

FOUNTAIN SCHOOL, SIXTH GRADE, 1933. Miss Whitehurst was the teacher. (Courtesy of Libbie Clayborne.)

PORTER TOWN/EASTERN PINES, 1930s. Fourth and fifth grade classes were taught in a two-room schoolhouse. The teacher was Hazel Cherry. Identified in this picture is fourth-grader Thelma Edwards (fifth from left). (Courtesy of Thelma Flye.)

1932 GRADUATION AT EAST CAROLINA TEACHERS COLLEGE, GREENVILLE. Students walked in formation close to Fifth Street while parents and faculty watched. (Courtesy of UA, ECU.)

BETHEL HIGH SCHOOL, BETHEL, 1937. The students include the following: Garland Whitehurst, Margaret Barnhill, Bertha Brown, Harrison W. Guess, Margaret Moore, Ivey Whitehurst, Annie Marie Dixon, Vera Edmonson, Francis Andrews, Dorothy Dean Bowers, Mildred Briley, Marjorie Williamson, Josephine Whitehurst, Cleo Beverley, Walter C. Latham, Marjorie Whitehurst, Earline Manning, Annie Gertrude Davenport, Jennie Louise Meeks, Francis Simon, Tyrae Allen Baker, Miss Frances Patrick, Vivian McLawhorn, Frank Bowers, Robert Burton, and Willie Abeyounis. (Courtesy of John Watson Sr.)

Front row —
Mary Allen, Myrtle Roth, Johann, Alice, Janice Sessions, Lucy

J.H. Rose High School on Fifth and Cotanche Streets in Greenville, 1944. Miss Schindler's homeroom class posed on the school steps. (Courtesy of Hazel Eden.)

A Distant View of J.H. Rose High School, Greenville, 1940s. (Courtesy of ECMC, ECU.)

SEVENTH GRADE CLASS, EAST CAROLINA TEACHERS COLLEGE, TRAINING SCHOOL, GREENVILLE, 1946. These students and faculty in front of Messick Building include the following: Bette Jane Bunch, James R. Robinson, Billy Wolfork, Barbara White, Mary Ann Waldrop, Frances Sigmon, Jackie Sears Violet, Dot Tucker, Virginia Perkins, Lyman Ormand, Carl Worsley, Carolyn Clapp, Mrs. Keeter, Ralph Smiley, Johnny Aman, Ann Sutton, Suggie Sugg; Catherine Clark, Joe Clark, and Miss Wahl. In 1959, the school would be renamed the Wahl-Coates School after Dora Coates and Frances Wahl, who were teachers and supervisors of the school during its formative years. (Courtesy of Dorothy Tucker Taft.)

SECOND GRADE CLASS, THIRD STREET SCHOOL, GREENVILLE, 1946. (Courtesy of Thelma Flye.)

FIRST GRADE CLASS, WEST GREENVILLE ELEMENTARY SCHOOL, 1962. (Courtesy of Ramona Tucker.)

L.H. ROBINSON UNION SCHOOL, WINTERVILLE, 1956. The faculty included Pauline Anderson, Bettie Pearl Carney, Pearl Gardner, Georgia Bush, Mary Monk, Beatrice Maye, Lena Spells, Carrie Best, Mabel Lang, Thelma Warren, Eleanor Vines, John Maye, Samuel Hemby, Roderick Harrel, and Moses Kennedy. (Courtesy of ECMC, ECU.)

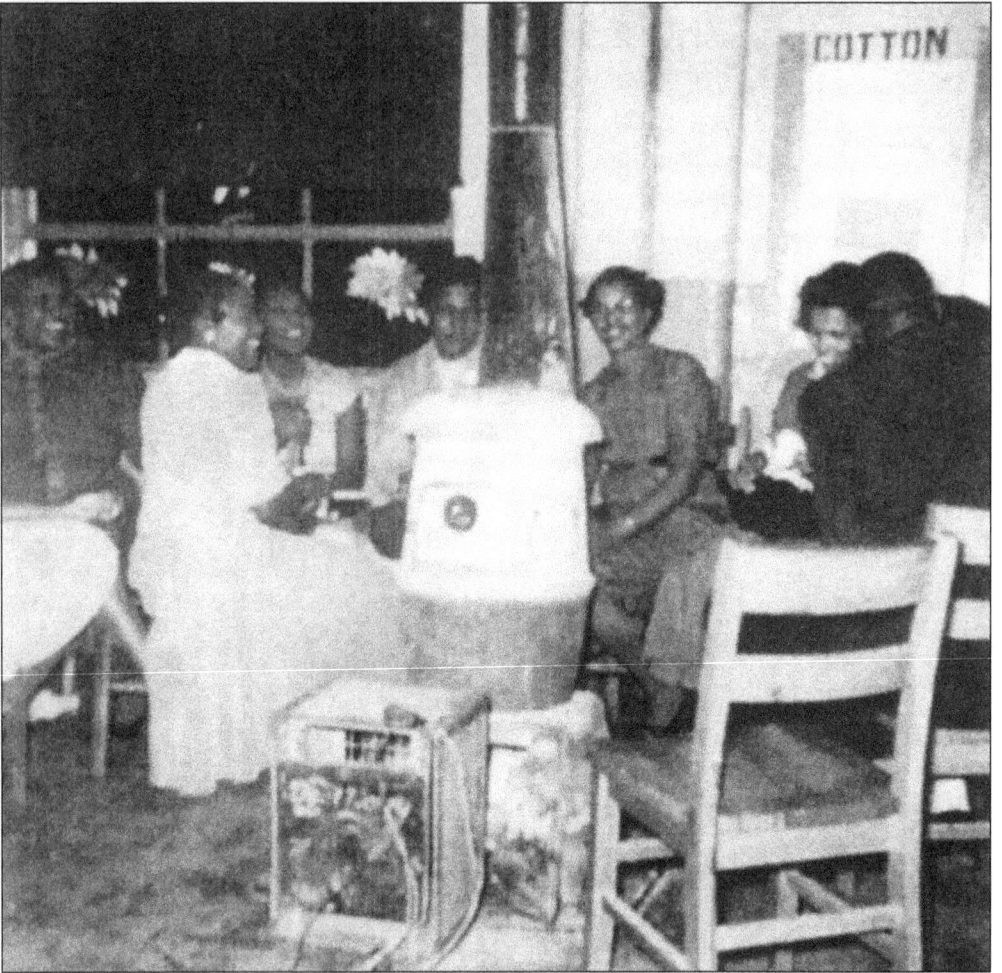

LES HOMMES, 1957. This group was a social club for professional men and women, and it met in J.J. Brown's Agricultural Shop at South Ayden High School in Ayden. Some of the members include Clara Best, Mary Forman, Beatrice Maye, and Clotea Garrett. (Courtesy of ECMC, ECU.)

Five

Churches

SUNDAY SERVICE AT RED BANKS PRIMITIVE CHURCH, SOUTH OF GREENVILLE, C. 1900. (Courtesy of Jean Tucker Joyner.)

CHRISTIAN CHURCH (DISCIPLES OF CHRIST) ON DICKINSON AVENUE, GREENVILLE, 1908. The church was destroyed in a fire, and in 1916, it was rebuilt in blond brick on Eighth Street near Dickinson Avenue. (Courtesy of Virginia Perkins.)

EMMANUEL EPISCOPAL CHURCH, FARMVILLE, c. 1920. In this view, work is being done on the spire. (Courtesy of ECMC, ECU.)

EIGHTH STREET CHRISTIAN CHURCH, GREENVILLE, 1940s. This was the Disciples of Christ Church after it was rebuilt on Eighth Street near Dickinson Avenue. (Courtesy of Hazel Eden.)

St. Peter's Catholic Church, Located on 107 West Second Street in Greenville, 1966. An earlier wooden building was purchased from St. Paul's Episcopal Church in 1885 and moved from Pitt Street next to Cherry Hill Cemetery to West Second Street. This brick building was built on site in the 1920s and was later torn down in the urban renewal project of 1966. The congregation moved to East Fifth Street. (Courtesy of ECMC, ECU.)

Memorial Baptist Church in Greenville. The church was constituted in 1827 with 23 members with Reverend Thomas Mason serving as their pastor. The structure seen here was their second building, which was erected in 1883–1884 and located at 313 South Greene Street. In 1973, they dedicated their present church on Greenville Boulevard.

SYCAMORE HILL BAPTIST CHURCH, LOCATED ON GREENE AND PITT STREETS BETWEEN THIRD AND FOURTH STREETS IN GREENVILLE. The building burned in 1968, and the congregation built a blond brick church in the 200 block of West Eighth Street. Recently, they have built a new church on Hooker Road. (Courtesy of ECMC, ECU.)

ARTHUR NORCOTT. A graduate of Greenville High School, Arthur Norcott studied music under Pashal Hearnes and Professor J.H. Killingsworth at Clark University. He later became the organist and musical director at Sycamore Hill Baptist Church in Greenville for 57 years. Mr. Norcott died in 1975. (Courtesy of ECMC, ECU.)

Six

Pastimes

KING CHILDREN IN FRONT OF THE PLAYHOUSE IN THEIR YARD AT 600 DICKINSON AVENUE IN GREENVILLE, 1901. The children are, from left to right, as follows: Elias (five months old), Annie (age five), Mattie Moye (age nine), and Richard (age two). (Courtesy of Virginia Perkins.)

RICHARD KING (RIGHT) AND FRED TAYLOR GOING FOR A DRIVE IN A MULE CART IN FRONT OF BOB GREENE'S HOUSE, GREENVILLE, 1906. (Courtesy of Virginia Perkins.)

JAMES "JIMMY" HARVEY WARD, BETHEL, c. 1910. Here, Jimmy is dressed for a recital with his piccolo banjo. These adapted instruments were all the rage from the 1890s through the 1920s, when entire orchestras of them performed. (Courtesy of Janice White Koonce.)

WHITE'S THEATRE

SAMUEL T. WHITE, Manager and Owner

GREENVILLE, NORTH CAROLINA

Seating Capacity 680
One Night Stands. High Class Vaudeville
and Good Pictures

WHITE'S THEATER, LOCATED AT 114 WEST FIFTH STREET IN GREENVILLE, C. 1920. The first movie theater in Greenville, White's Theater opened in 1914 with seating for 680 people. Acts at the theater included traveling companies known as one-night stands, high-class vaudeville, and good pictures. It was owned by Samuel Tilden White. (Courtesy of ECMC, ECU.)

NORTH CAROLINA EASTERN EXPOSITION, FARMVILLE, 1920. The exposition included a parade with floats by a variety of civic organizations. (Courtesy of ECMC, ECU.)

PLAYTIME, BETHEL, 1920s. Remember cartwheels and standing on your hands? (Courtesy of Janice White Koonce.)

THE BABY PARADE, SPRING/EASTER, FARMVILLE, 1920s. Mothers always want to get out of the house and babies love to explore, so springtime is a natural season for the event. (Courtesy of the May Museum.)

RALPH C. TUCKER SR. (ON THE RUNNING BOARD) AND WILL TUCKER AT THE WHEEL OF HIS WILLIS KNIGHT AUTOMOBILE, SOUTH OF GREENVILLE, 1926. (Courtesy of Ralph C. Tucker Sr.)

PLEASURE-RIDING HORSE IN THE WINTER SNOW, FARMVILLE AREA, 1927. The horse, named Baby, belonged to Tabitha DeVisconti and was kept on Larry C. Tugwell's Woodland farm. (Courtesy of the May Museum.)

JOHN M. GODWIN, GREENVILLE, 1938. John is seen here enjoying his goat cart in front of his house at 1012 Ward Street. Goat carts were something of a vogue for pictures of children. (Courtesy of Jeanne Jenkins.)

CECIL CLAYBORNE, PITT COUNTY, 1938. Guitar in hand and leaning on the back of his car, Cecil Clayborne is ready to sing. (Courtesy of Libbie Clayborne.)

OLIVIA WARD AND HER SISTER, CLARA WARD ROBERSON, PLAYING IN THE SNOW, BETHEL, 1936. (Courtesy of Janice White Koonce.)

LILLIAN EARLE EDWARDS IN FRONT OF THE PACK HOUSE ACROSS THE ROAD FROM THE EDWARDS FARM, PORTER TOWN, 1940s. Every Saturday night the pack house was used for square dancing. (Courtesy of Thelma Flye.)

HAYWOOD DAIL LAUGHINGHOUSE JR. WITH HIS 1941 CHEVY CONVERTIBLE, PACTOLUS, 1941. Automobiles from 1941 were the last models made until the end of World War II. The convertible's top was entirely automatic. (Courtesy of Haywood Dail Laughinghouse Jr.)

RALPH C. TUCKER SR. AND HIS 1946 PONTIAC IN FRONT OF JIMMY WELLS SERVICE STATION ON THE CORNER OF GREENE AND FOURTH STREETS, GREENVILLE, 1946. (Courtesy of Ralph C. Tucker Sr.)

PITCH A BOOGIE WOOGIE. *Pitch a Boogie Woogie* was a musical production filmed in Greenville in 1948 by John Warner using a local cast. This show was the first movie made by a production company that was based in North Carolina. It was popular in the Carolinas until the production company, Lord-Warner, dissolved the following year. The movie was never shown outside of the Carolinas. (Courtesy of ECMC, ECU.)

KING BROTHERS COMBINED CIRCUS, GREENVILLE, 1954. Everybody loves the circus. Performers would set up their camp north of town for the duration of their stay. European circuses during the nineteenth century generally stayed in a permanent location. During the last century, the United States was made up primarily of small rural populations that could not maintain a circus in one location. To meet the demand for entertainment, circuses traveled throughout the country. (Courtesy of ECMC, ECU.)

CIRCUS. The American circus developed an advertising gimmick to heighten interest of people to come and see the acts. Once camp was set up, the circus always had a parade through the business district of town. It was free publicity, enticement to the children, and fun for the whole family. In 1954, the King Brothers Combined Circus paraded down West Fourth Street with animals and clowns, encouraging people to come out to the ring and see the show under the big top with all its death-defying and precision acts, marvel at the wide variety of animals, and just have a good time.

www.ingramcontent.com/pod-product-compliance
Lightning Source LLC
Chambersburg PA
CBHW082146150426
42812CB00076B/1929